**leeclowsbeard**

 leeclowsbeard

by @leeclowsbeard

 powerHouse Books

Brooklyn, NY

BABY STE
ARE FOR
NOT BRA
BE AMAZ
BE SURPA

PS
BABIES,
DS.
NG OR
SSED.

7:46 am Mar 2nd 2010

CONSUMERS NEVER COMPLAIN ABOUT ADS BEING TOO SMART.

7:46 am Aug 17th 2009

An ad should say one thing well. Now here are fifty-three bullet points why.

7:03 am May 12th 2009

Your ad begins as an interruption. Make paying attention to it feel like a reward.

7:55 am May 14th 2009

Art direction is part of a brand's voice. So consider not using Trajan Pro this time.

6:15 am May 15th 2009

A technique or look is no substitute for substance.

6:47 am May 18th 2009

TV spots are short. If you can't hold folks' attention for 20 secs before revealing the brand, find another line of work.

8:05 am May 19th 2009

Never underestimate the intelligence of your audience. The subtleties of value-priced hemorrhoid cream are lost on few.

6:34 am May 20th 2009

It's called a creative brief, not a copy-and-paste brief.

6:30 am May 21st 2009

It's the little compromises that add up to a giant bucket of suck.

6:26 am May 22nd 2009

PUSH
"I'll trash your ads,
you take care of
your magazines
and newspapers."
—Lee

TOO MANY PEOPLE THINK THE THINGS THAT ARE EASY ABOUT ADVERTISING ARE HARD, AND VICE VERSA.

6:21 am May 26th 2009

One list of bullet points does not equal a "single, most-persuasive message."

7:34 am May 27th 2009

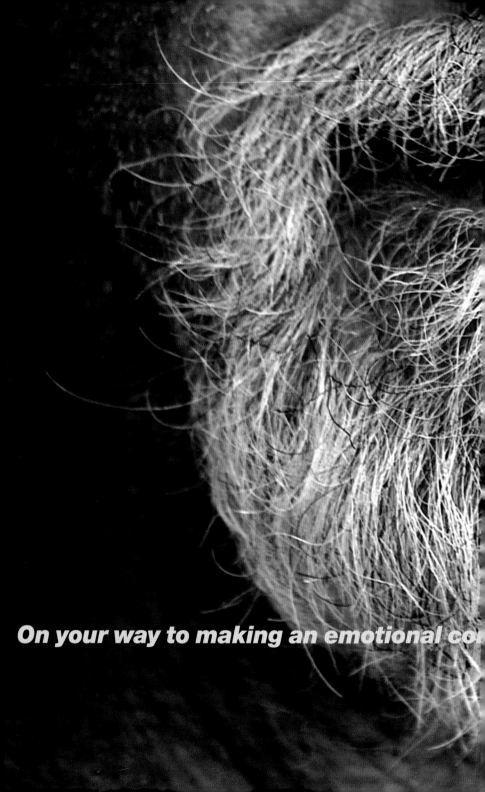

On your way to making an emotional co

tion, don't bypass the intellectual one.

6:40 am Jul 6th 2009

no one reads body copy, why are we on round 13 of client visions? 6:26 am Sep 10th 2009 Budgets don't constrict ideas

ey hone. 6:37 am Sep 8th 2009 From mass to social, media is nsumed by individuals. Speak accordingly. 8:16 am Aug 19th

An ad discussing negative things does not a negative ac ike, e.g., every problem-solution ad ever run. 6:59 am Sep 1s

Beat up the brief before it gets approved, or it will beat u up when you're trying to get work approved. 6:52 am Aug 24th

The love of money is the root of much bad advertising.

am Sep 9th 2009 It's not that consumers have short attentior ans. It's that we give them so little of interest to look at. 7:5

Aug 26th 2009 Thank a media person today. After all, no one nembers an ad they never see. 8:49 am Aug 27th 2009 Every int wants something new. And three examples of where

worked before. 6:38 am Aug 28th 2009 Media runs from free to pensive. But your idea should always be rich. (This is less vious as you may think.) 7:54 am Aug 31st 2009 Dearest bywriter, please thoroughly learn your native tongue before u butcher it for advertising. 6:54 am Sep 3rd 2009 Dear client, Glad u believe advertising can do a lot for your brand. Just nember "a lot" is a far cry from "everything." 6:48 am Sep 4th 2009

vertising is always transitory and often disposable. We can y prevent people from becoming the latter. 7:32 am Sep 11th 2009

Media changes. The rules of good creative do not.

6:36 am May 28th 2009

6:48 am Sep 2nd 2009

LAST I CHECK

"SNARKY IRO

NOT THE APP

VOICE FOR 9

THE WORLD'S

,
Y" IS
OPRIATE
% OF
RANDS.

A GENUINE UNIQUE SELLING STYLE BEATS A

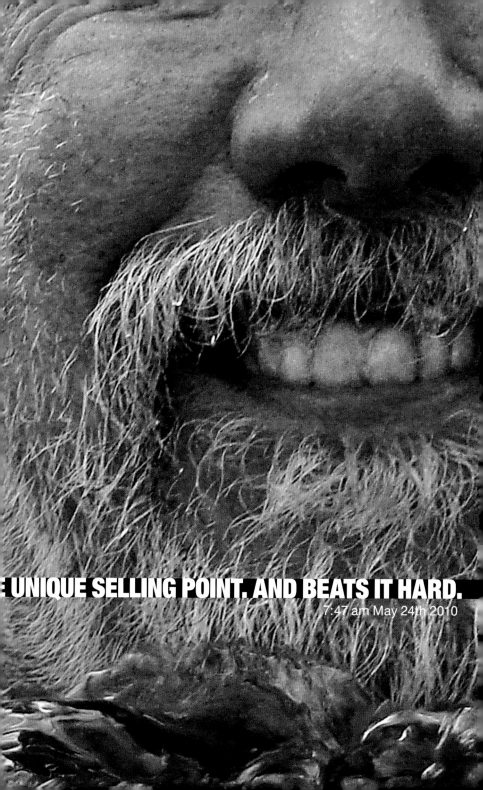

UNIQUE SELLING POINT. AND BEATS IT HARD.

7:47 am May 24th 2010

—

6:58 am Jun 23rd 2

THIS APPLIES TO BRANDS AND PEOPLE ALIKE: IF YOU HAVE NOTHING TO SAY, DON'T. BETTER TO REMAIN MYSTERIOUS THAN BE ANNOYING.

When someone says, "I wouldn't fall on my sword for that," ask if they've fallen on a sword for anything. Ever.

8:29 am Oct 13th 2009

A big idea transcends budgets

But a big budget never hurt a transcendent idea.

7:16 am Jun 23rd 2010

If ROI only means bumping tomorrow's numbers, the spammers have already won.

6:23 am July 14th 2009

Try asking your doctor to do a little angioplasty on spec.

7:12 am Jul 16th 2009

Dear Asst. AE, Please stop sending PDFs to the client with the closing, "Let me know if there are any more changes." - LCB

8:12 am Jul 17th 2009

"What do you think?" is not code for "What's wrong with this?"

7:54 am Jul 20th 2009

Don't confuse a simple execution with a simple message.
The former is optional; the latter, mandatory.

6:55 am Jul 23rd 2009

If your campaign's sole means of measuring success is a coupon code, it's already failed.

7:00 am Jul 27th 2009

If you undermine the creative—either the work or the team—with the clien I'll undermine you with HR.

7:55 am Jul 28th 2009

Learning to phrase "doing that would be stupid and wrong" in a way tha makes the client smile is a skill worth mastering.

9:20 am Jul 29th 2009

Do you remember the last bullet point you read? Me neither.
Impact requires craft.

6:35 am Jul 30th 2009

"But some people won't get this" is one of the first signs your ad might actually work.

7:51 am Jul 31st 2009

The only action you can bore someone into is ignoring you.

6:36 am Aug 3rd 2009

Advertising is 95% less subjective than most account people would have you believe. But that's just my opinion.

6:39 am Aug 4th 2009

"We can do a million ads like this" should never be uttered by someone who's yet to write a single one.

6:28 am Aug 5th 2009

Being "direct" is not the same as being persuasive.

10:47 am Aug 6th 2009

Shouting will garner you a lot of attention, but few friends

If you want a stronger call to action, create a better ad.

6:33 am Jul 22nd 2009

8:30 am Sep 14th 2009

If a client doesn't deserve your best thinking, why are they your client?

Few things break my heart like seeing a brilliant idea poorly executed. Always sweat the details.

9:10 am Jun 11th 2009

Writers should be able to articulately defend design, and vice versa.

6:31 am Jun 15th 2009

Great ideas can come from anywhere.
Even creatives.

5:50 am Jun 16th 2009

Always read your copy out loud to ensure it sounds like the brand and not the brand manager.

6:40 am Jun 19th 2009

Advertising is not about self-expression, it's about brand-expression. But if you can work in a bit of the former, do it.

5:57 am Jun 22nd 2009

While frustrating, clients don't have to explain why they hate something. Account folks, CDs and your partner do.

6:31 am Jun 24th 2009

If you'd put it in a PowerPoint deck, don't put it in your ad.

6:24 am Jun 25th 2009

Saying as little as possible–in advertising and real life–covers a multitude of sins.
6:04 am Jun 30th 2009

Clients are consumers, too. They just need to be reminded. Often.
6:17 am Jul 1st 2009

Consumers really don't care about your paradigm shifting. Relevancy will always be king.
6:40 am Jul 2nd 2009

The consumer will never hear that two-hour campaign rationale you gave to the client. Work lives or dies on its own merits.
8:54 am Jul 8th 2009

Hope you like that straw dog because the client just approved it.
9:26 am Jul 9th 2009

YOU CAN'T FIX A STRATEGY IN POST.
6:46 am Jul 10th 2009

If at first you don't succeed, a lifestyle photo is not the solution.
7:01 am Jul 13th 2009

The number of days spent on a brief should equal the number of weeks creatives get to concept. Not vice versa.
7:10 am Aug 14th 2009

BEFORE SUGGESTI[
FIRST ASK, "AM I M[
OR MERELY DIFFER[

6:23 am Oct 29th 2009

Given the choice, I'd rather push the brand than the envelope.

8:09 am Jul 7th 2009

LIKE ALL STORYTELLING, GR
ARCHETYPICAL STRUCTURE
DRESS YOUR BRAND APPRO

T ADVERTISING DRESSES
N ALLURING NEW CLOTHES.
ATELY.

If it
needs
to be
buried
in the
body
copy, it
needs
to be
buried
altogether

am Jul 15th 2009

We have nothing to fea

...t fearful clients. 7:34 am May 28th 2010

Dearest account sup: It's not that the client's sugge

8:26 am Aug 21st 2009

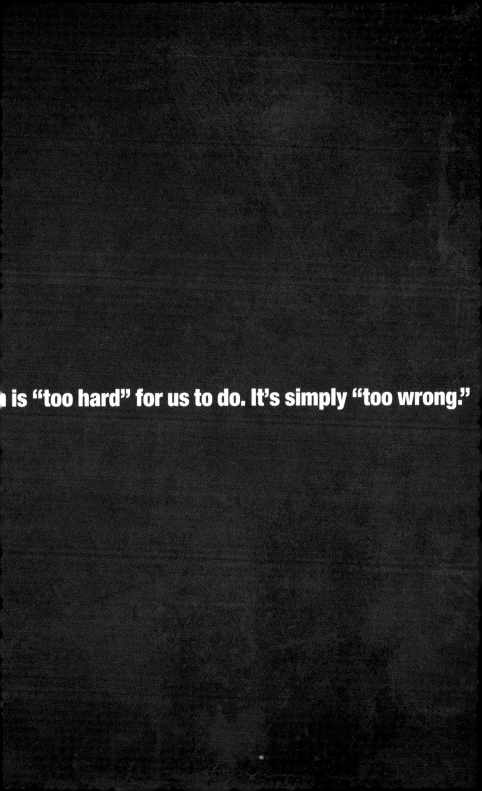

is "too hard" for us to do. It's simply "too wrong."

he client may be the judge,
ut the consumer is the jury and executioner.
5 am Dec 1st 2010

Ideas
are only
as fragile
as the
backbones
behind
them.

32 am Nov 23rd 2009

Copy & design
internal rhyth
can't describe
know when th

create an ad's
. Even if they
t, consumers
beat is off. 11:26 am Oct 2nd 2009

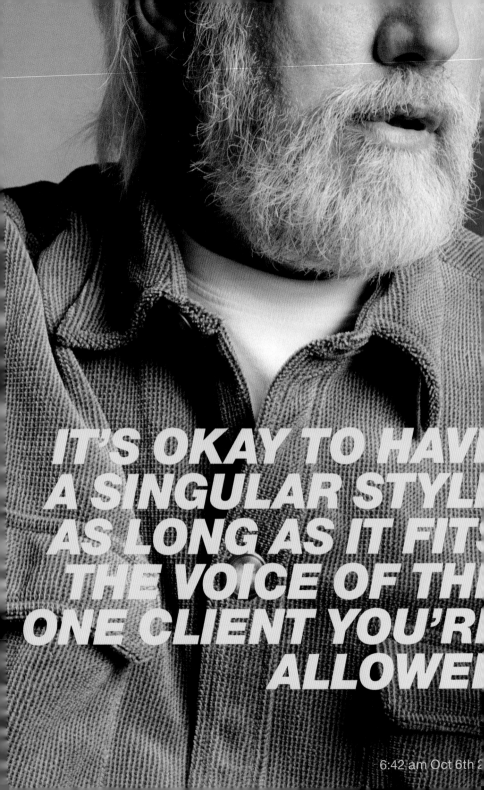

IT'S OKAY TO HAVE
A SINGULAR STYLE
AS LONG AS IT FITS
THE VOICE OF THE
ONE CLIENT YOU'RE
ALLOWED

6:42 am Oct 6th 2

'O WORK ON.

The person or beard who can quantify revenue lost by bad client mandates will be rich overnight. And dead in a week.

6:50 am Sep 15th 2009

The biggest waste of time and money in most agencies is the inability to make a decision. Lead yourselves. Lead your clients.

7:32 am Sep 16th 2009

Just because everyone (ad folks) is doing it, doesn't mean anyone (consumers) actually likes it.

6:58 am Sep 18th 2009

Colorful ideas rarely come from beige cubicles.

8:09 am Sep 21st 2009

Effective advertising makes the familiar seem new and the new seem familiar.

7:19 am Sep 22nd 2009

Don't confuse tools with strategies. (cough) SEO optimization. (cough) Twitter. (cough cough)

8:01 am Sep 23rd 2009

Resource management tip: "Good enough" is good enough when it's better than most others' best.

7:23 am Sep 25th 2009

Brevity is the soul of status meetings. And that soul has been hunted down and beaten with a stick.

8:50 am Sep 28th 2009

"Did you consider trying this?" No, we're good enough to reject it without wasting time trying it. Your CFO will thank us.

Pointing out another's idea reeks is not evidence that yours is genius.
7:29 am Mar 30th 2010

Hard to blame clients for not being conceptual when we keep showing them computer comps and ripomatics.
7:58 am Mar 31st 2010

The best insights usually make you feel like you should've known them all along.
8:21 am Apr 1st 2010

Only ads for upcoming Gov't Mule shows should be jam-packed.
8:02 am Apr 5th 2010

The easiest, best and (in the long run) cheapest way to mitigate risk in advertising is to simply let great people do their jobs.
7:36 am Apr 8th 2010

Just because most of us would be creative for free doesn't mean we should be expected to.
7:13 am Apr 12th 2010

Our job is to communicate complex things simply. Let's start with this brief, shall we?
7:08 am Apr 14th 2010

People only learn everything about a brand through experience. Again, that's "experience," not "banner ad."
7:37 am Mar 19th 2010

I've yet to hire a writer who uses ellipses in an ad.

If contrary to a brand's personality, a limited-time offer can cause lasting damage.

10:00 am Oct 26th 2010

Creative that reflects the brand's voice means little if the media placement doesn't do likewise.

8:03 am Oct 28th 2010

Telling people they're going to love something is a sure signal they probably won't.

8:30 am Nov 2nd 2010

While "it" and "something" can both be anything, "just do it" is everything "just do something" is not. See, copy does matter.

8:22 am Nov 3rd 2010

I see your estimate barely allows for shallow thinking and shoddy execution. Let's rework those numbers, shall we?

8:17 am Nov 4th 2010

If you come up with an idea Friday afternoon and it still sounds good Monday morning, run with it.

12:19 pm Nov 5th 2010

If it's important enough to say it with an ad, it's important enough to say it without a pun.

8:25 am Nov 9th 2010

A literal mind is a terrible thing to waste time with.

10:30 am Nov 11th 2010

Your mission is to create a transient message that makes a lasting impression. Godspeed.

8:09 am Nov 12th 2010

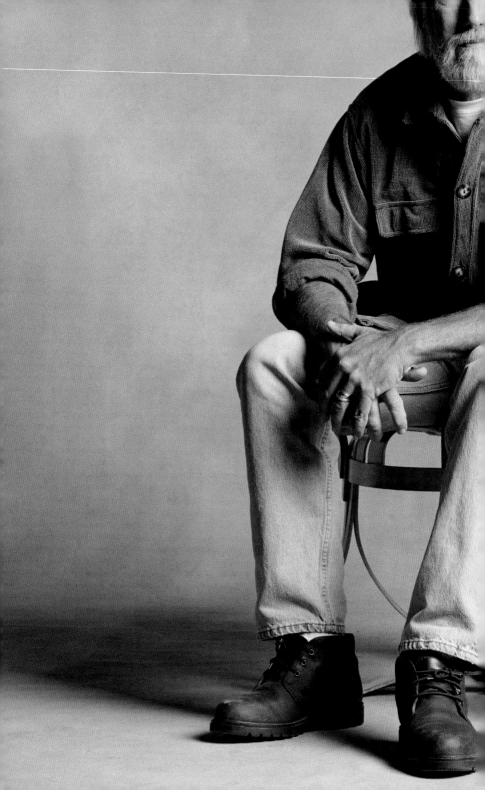

It's easier to get great work when you treat great people with great respect.

8:23 am Oct 7th 2009

7:02 am Oct 7th 2

WHAT WILL
YOU DO
WHEN
EVERYONE
IS SEO
OPTIMIZED?
OH RIGHT,
GO
BACK
TO
IDEAS.

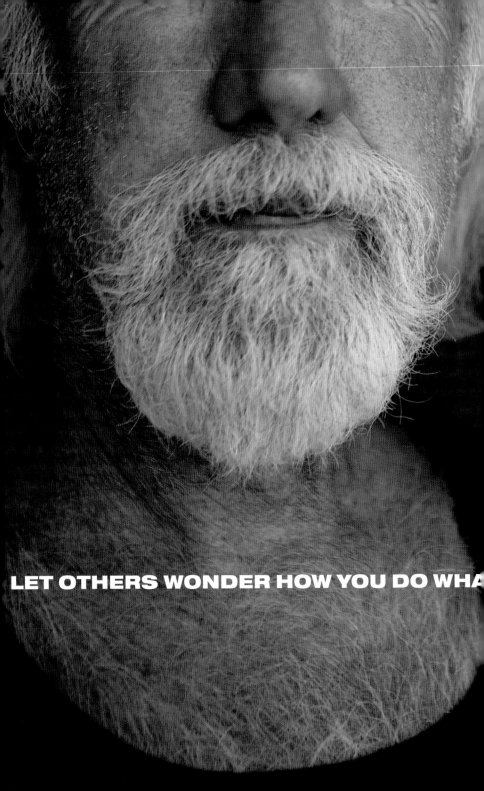

LET OTHERS WONDER HOW YOU DO WHA

OU DO. JUST BE THANKFUL YOU CAN.

6:57 am Jul 22nd 2010

WORRY ABOUT

THE
IMPRESSION
AN AD WILL
MAKE BEFORE
WORRYING
ABOUT
HOW MANY
IMPRESSIONS
IT WILL GET.

10 am Oct 14th 2010

The best clients are rarely easy to please because they're or eased by the same things we are.

THE MORE
INDECISIVE
CLIENT, T
OPTIONS T
SHOULD S

THE

FEWER

HEY

E.

Before you decree a standard for others, make sure you can meet it yourself.

The greatest obstacle most agencies and clients must overcome is the inertia of their own internal ways.

Guess what? Your style guide isn't your brand, either.

When people work together intelligently, the incessant need to tear down silos suddenly goes away.

The more mass the media, the more singular the message.

If you're thinking about being a thought leader, you're doing it wrong.

Many things bear repeating. Just not during every commercial break.

Consumers ultimately decide what a compelling offer is, despite what Kent in merchandising says.

Plain speech works great in ads and even better in presentations.

If you're always exceeding clients' expectations, you may just be working for some fairly mediocre clients.

9:10 am Aug 18th 2010

3:21 am Aug 19th 2010

3:57 am Aug 20th 2010

9:23 am Aug 23rd 2010

3:02 am Aug 25th 2010

7:56 am Aug 26th 2010

7:49 am Aug 27th 2010

3:03 am Aug 30th 2010

7:59 am Aug 31st 2010

**"Hard to explain"
is vastly different than
"hard to get."**

11:29 am Feb 9th 2010

f we have to
it the message
nto a 30-sec
spot or 40k
banner, you
can fit the brief
nto 1 page.

5 am Nov 13th 2009

No man is wise who refuses to risk.

8:51 am Aug 9th 2010

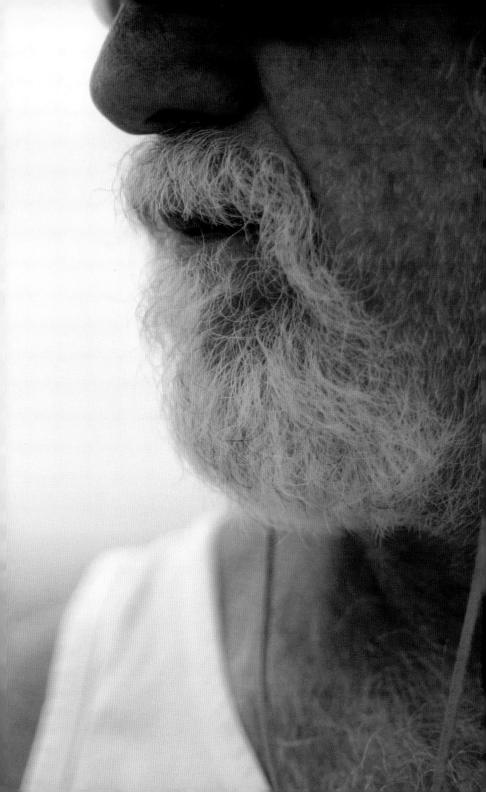

A BRAND'S VOICE CAN BE PLAINSPOKEN WITHOUT BEING PLAIN.

:33 am Jul 12th 2010

I'll let you move the logo from the bottom right when you can explain why it is usually there in the first place.
8:45 am Nov 16th 2009

You should always focus group creative, assuming your goal is creative that satisfies 30 people.
6:39 am Nov 17th 2009

Most people don't have enough time to interact with their kids, let alone your brand. Respect that.
8:20 am Nov 18th 2009

Ask "why" when digging for insights. Ask "why not" when reviewing creative.
6:19 am Nov 19th 2009

The better the work, the shorter the case study.
6:55 am Nov 20th 2009

Agencies would be better places to work if we celebrated what went right as much as we analyze what went wrong.
6:41 am Nov 24th 2009

An ad that's universally liked hasn't been shown to everyone yet.
9:51 am Nov 27th 2009

Though often questioned or ignored, be thankful for the talent with which you are blessed. It's better than the alternative.

6:11 am Nov 25th 2009

In the end, an ad with many messages has one message: Ignore me.

Wednesday is too late to use the term "later this

6:52 am Dec 2nd 2009 In our hunt for novelty, we forget th

already consider it novel. 6:49 am Dec 4th 2009 Face time

to work on an inspiring brand to create inspired ac

"What are we trying to say with this ad" should be

showing the client. 7:59 am Dec 11th 2009 Always give cre

"take" in that sentence. 7:20 am Dec 15th 2009 If your copy re

ek" unless you think the week ends on Monday.

reat advertising is so rarely seen that consumers

substitute for idea time. 6:53 am Dec 8th 2009 If you need

ising, you picked the wrong career. 12:27 pm Dec 10th 2009

ed before writing the brief. Not two minutes before

here credit is due. Note the absence of the word

s italics, your copy requires rewriting. 7:21 am Dec 16th 2009

Dear Jr. AE,
"Question everything"
on your own time,
not during a client
presentation.
Love, LCB

6:46 am Dec 9th 2009

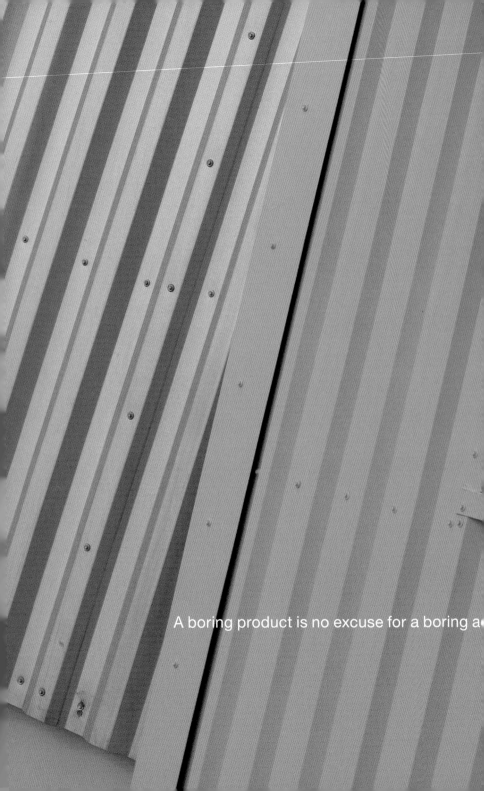

A boring product is no excuse for a boring a◀

SPEND

HOUR

RATIONA

AN E

THE

IT'S A

NG THREE

GIVING A

LE ABOUT

MOTIONAL

MEDIUM IS

EFINITION

OF IRONY.

8:01 am Dec 14th 2009

SO DUMB.

GREAT ADVERTISING FEELS LIKE IT'S EVERYWHERE (IN A GOOD WAY) WITHOUT BEING EVERYWHERE. MAKE MEDIA PART OF THE CREATIVE PLAN.

8:28 am Aug 10th 2010

8:14 am Nov 16th 2C

e art of compromise includes knowing when not to.

OFTEN

THE MORE YOU SAY, THE LESS YOU'RE HEARD.

7:44 am Jan 7th 2010

You can't cut clutter with clutter.
8:09 am Nov 8th 2010

Make sure your brand's voice is one people outside the company actually want to hear.
6:42 am Nov 12th 2009

Always assume no one wants to hear what your ad has to say, then give them a reason to.
7:53 am Dec 21st 2009

Understanding that a single most-persuasive idea should not contain an "and" is apparently more difficult than I realized.
6:46 am Mar 24th 2010

In the ad game, "Well, we got it all in there," should always be said with a deep sense of shame.
7:48 am Apr 19th 2010

The next time someone says, "We want to do something viral," sneeze on him. Viral is a phenomenon, not a strategy.
7:57 am Apr 30th 2010

A logo that is 10% bigger won't help a message that is 50% irrelevant.
9:01 am Jul 6th 2011

Great advertising boosts the top line. Great agencies help boost the bottom, too.
7:59 am Aug 17th 2010

Creative-by-committee does not count as crowdsourcing.
7:42 am May 17th 2010

Focus on what matters. The more you split hairs, the farther behind you fall.
8:02 am May 25th 2010

It's hard to solve clients' problems if you're always solving client problems.
8:33 am Jun 2nd 2010

Big thinkers don't mistake simple ideas for small ones.
8:29 am Jun 4th 2010

If your own work bores you, chances are you're not alone in that assessment.
8:28 am Jun 11th 2010

Yes, agencies are replaceable. But then, so are clients.
7:47 am Jun 14th 2010

Dear Client, Big thinking demands bold action. Please don't ask for the former if you fear the latter. Love, LCB
8:01 am Jun 28th 2010

Agencies that don't celebrate good work eventually stop producing any.
8:58 am Jul 1st 2010

Great advertising can transform a commodity into something captivating.
9:22 am Aug 13th 2010

I'd rather over promise and deliver just right.

HO
NTS
BE
%ING
ISING
NCY

An ad should be an

appetizer, not a buffet.

Dogs rule.

7:38 am Mar 25th 2010

IF YOU MUST CHOOSE
BETWEEN ANNOYING
A CLIENT OR ANNOYING
THEIR CUSTOMERS,
PICK THE FORMER.
THAT RELATIONSHIP IS
EASIER TO MEND.

8:07 am Apr 23rd 2010

White space makes any brief better.

7:04 am Feb 26th 2010

DEAR CLIENTS

IT'S OKAY
FOR YOU TO
EXCEED OUR
EXPECTATIONS,
TOO. *LOVE, LCB*

 8:06 am Sep 1st 2010

8:13 am Nov 23rd 2010

SOONER
IS BETTER THAN LATER,
BUT
IT'S NEVER
BETTER
THAN BETTER.

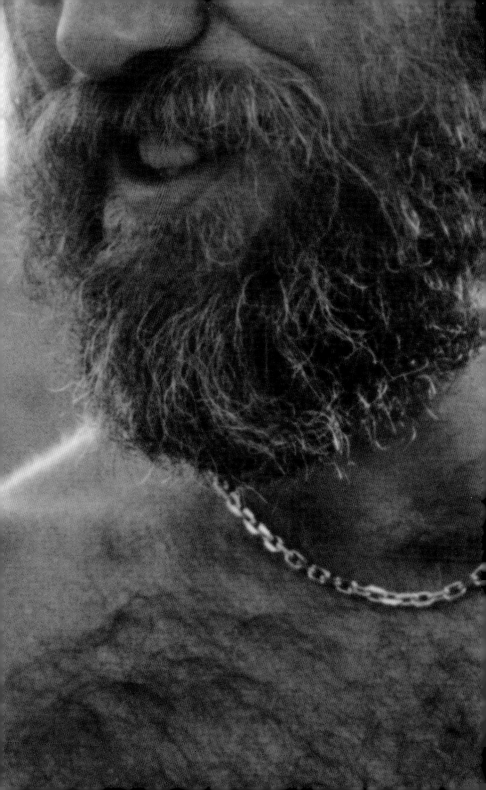

If there's no such thing as a bad idea

why do we have to
how the client three?
)am Dec 3rd 2009

7:57 am Aug 16th 2C

ght the proliferation of mediocrity.

A great ad says one thing

et accomplishes many.

7 am Apr 2nd 2010

The better the work the shorter the presentation

7:41 am Oct 9th 20

I love clients who know the difference between input and a mandate.

8:58 am Oct 8th 2009

You can't judge a book by its cover.
Unless it uses Wingdings.

6:01 am Oct 15th 2009

Dear Jr. (or Sr.) team: Before whining about not getting good work produced, try showing some first.

7:24 am Oct 19th 2009

Actually, we can afford the media buy if we take some $$ from your CYA testing budget.

6:20 am Oct 20th 2009

It takes artistry & craft to achieve objective results in a subjective medium. And no small amount of voodoo.

7:01 am Oct 21st 2009

When judging an ad internally, react like a consumer first and analyze it to death later. Like after it runs.

10:42 am Oct 22nd 2009

Dear new writer, there's a difference between being cynical and wry. Learn it before the next client meeting.

7:10 am Oct 23rd 2009

Too often, "make it more direct" is just code for "I don't get it."

6:52 am Oct 27th 2009

Great ads solve advertising problem
7:44 am May 4th 201

reat agencies solve business problems.

Your target
is *not the*
overzealous
client

t is the
ambivalent
consumer.

27 am Apr 22nd 2010

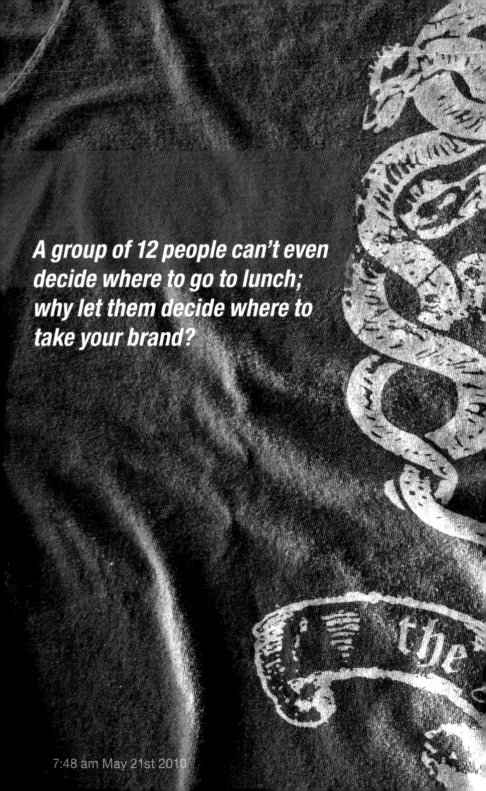

A group of 12 people can't even decide where to go to lunch; why let them decide where to take your brand?

7:48 am May 21st 2010

Dogs rule.

8:03 am Aug 24th 2

ctions speak louder than meetings.

This tweet has no call to action.
Yet you're reading it anyway, and
it reinforces the LCB brand.

Win. 7:46 am Feb 16th 2010

's called a presentation,
ot a PowerPoint read-a-long.

**ATTENTION
IS PAID WHE**

ATTENTION IS DESERVED.

8:57 am Sep 2nd 2010

GUEST

CREATIVITY CAN
MAKE ANY MESSAGE
INTERESTING.
IT CANNOT, HOWEVER,
MAKE EVERY MESSAGE
EFFECTIVE.

51 am Jul 26th 2010

...sign is often the difference between
...ing ignored and being embraced.

3 am Aug 12th 2010

THE ONLY FORM OF COMMUNICATION MO[

THE CORPORATE MISSION STATEMENT. 6:

TO STOP AND SMELL THE ROSES AND HO

THAT CONFERENCE CALL. 9:09 am Jan 25

INSIGHT. 7:16 am Jan 26th 2010 PREACHIN

Jan 27th 2010 WHILE THE % OF GOOD WRI

OF HARDHEADED WRITERS WHO ARE GO[

DON'T NEED ALL THE REASONS TO LO

AND A COUPON DOESN'T COUNT. 7:31 am J

FOR PSYCHOLOGICAL WARFARE. 7:57

WHEN YOU CAN STEAL IT OUTRIGHT.

"NIMBLE" HAS NOTHING TO DO WITH YO

EBULOUS THAN THE JOB CHANGE NOTE IS

Jan 21st 2010 **SOMETIMES YOU JUST HAVE**

E ENSUING SNEEZING GETS YOU OUT OF

10 **COMMON SENSE TRUMPS ALLEGED**

AY TEACH, BUT SHARING SELLS. 6:44 am

WHO ARE HARDHEADED IS HIGH, THE %

LOW. 6:49 am Jan 28th 2010 **CONSUMERS**

UR BRAND, JUST ONE REALLY GOOD ONE.

h 2010 **AN HONEST BRAND HAS LITTLE NEED**

b 3rd 2010 **NEVER BORROW INTEREST**

am Feb 10th 2010 **DEAREST AE, BEING**

DICROUS TIMELINES. 7:06 am Feb 11th 2010

Make your brand the strong call to actio

3 am Dec 15th 2010

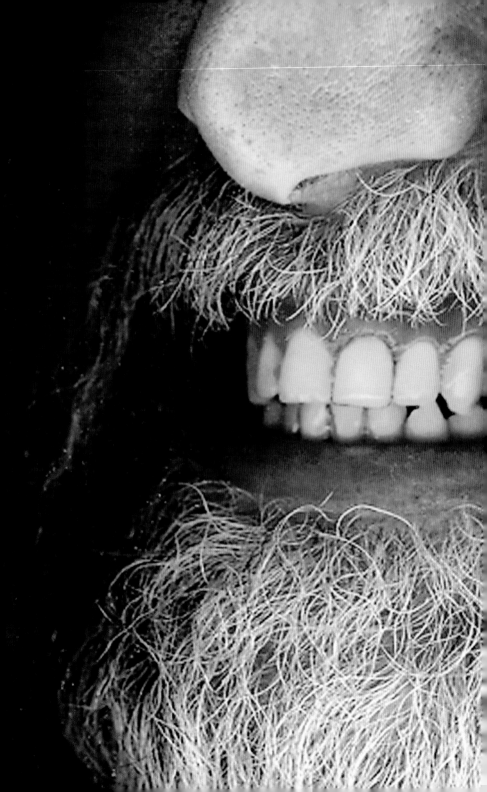

For what it costs in time wasted,
ideas stunted and work undermined,
talk is anything but cheap.
Speak wisely out there.

7:38 am Aug 5th 2010

{Making ant
client chang
actually pre
work does
as proactive

cipated
es before
enting the
ot count
thinking.} 8:00 am Feb 19th 2010

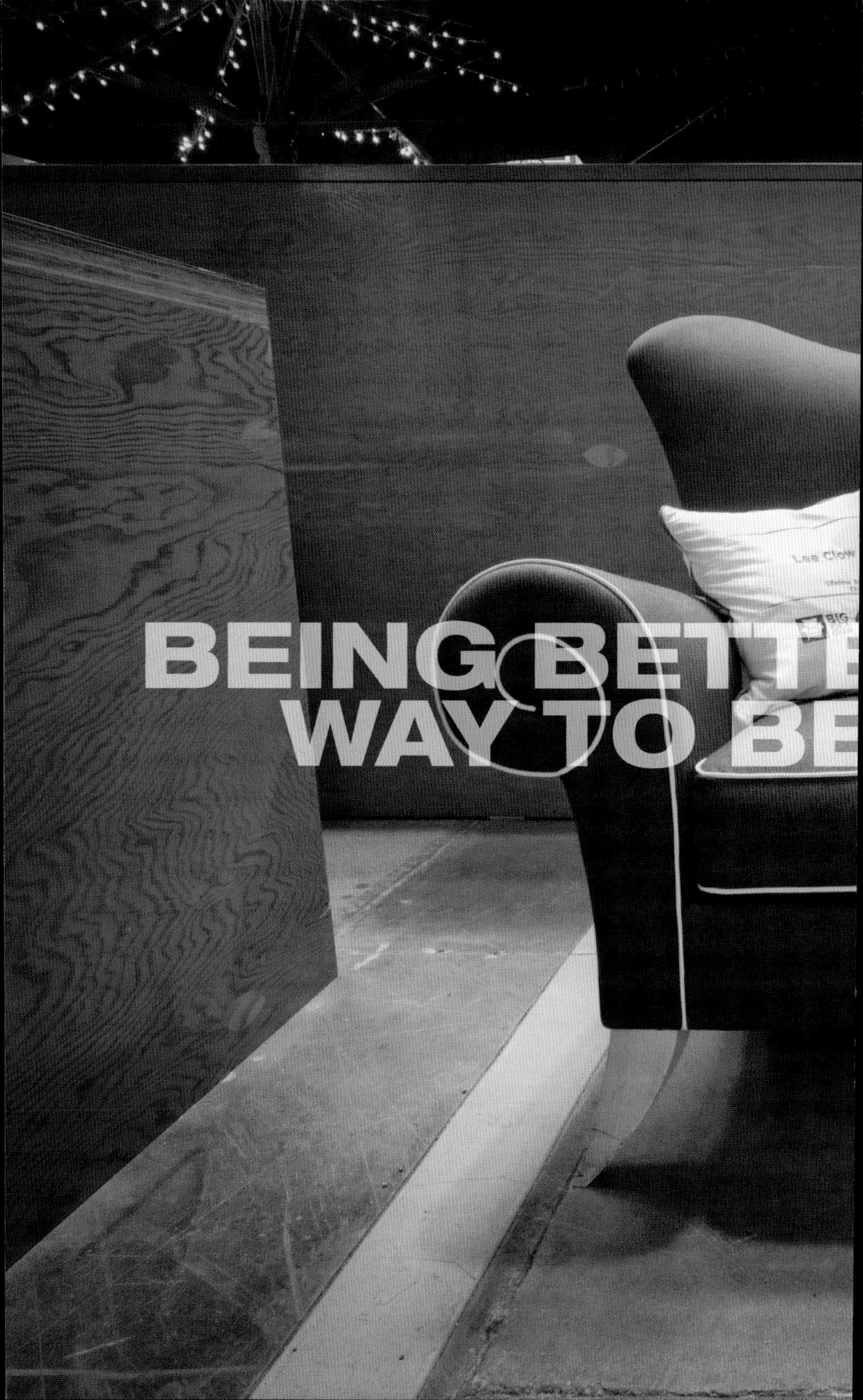

BEING BETTE
WAY TO BE

R IS THE BEST
DIFFERENT.

8:05 am Nov 30th 2010

IN MATTERS OF STORYTELLING, "FRESH" USUALLY TRUMPS "ORIGINAL."

FEW THINGS GUARANTEE FAILURE FASTER THAN THE "SAFE" OPTION.

6:58 am Nov 9th 2009

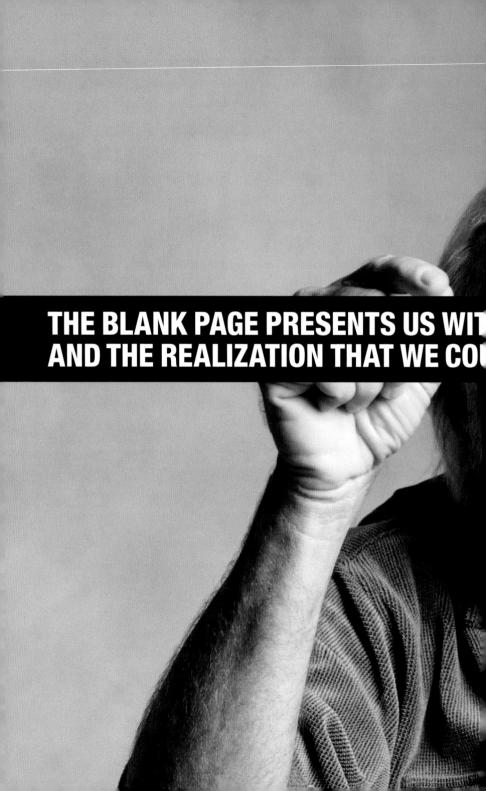

THE BLANK PAGE PRESENTS US WIT[H]
AND THE REALIZATION THAT WE CO[U]

IFINITE CREATIVE OPPORTUNITIES
REALLY USE A BRIEF. 9:15 am Sep 29th 2009

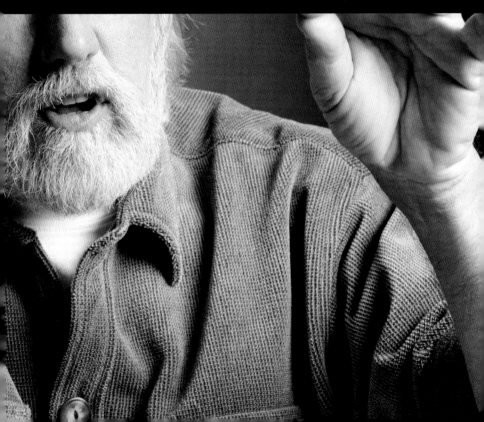

8:18 am Nov 29th 2010

If you're not promoting a truth, you're accelerating a failure.

'Tis the season to work on being a better person. Not a better personal brand.
9:50 am Dec 24th 2009

The ad world has little use for an unobservant copywriter.
8:27 am Jan 5th 2010

Ads need two things: A reason to pay attention and a reason to be glad attention was paid.
8:44 am Jan 6th 2010

Dearest client, in the spirit of the season, we're donating
7:57 am Dec 23rd 2009

People who eat, sleep and breathe advertising are rarely gr
7:32 am Jan 8th 2010

"[Blank] is the new [blank]" is grounds for immediate floggi
6:25 am Jan 11th 2010

Sometimes work makes the client nervous because it's b
6:38 am Jan 11th 2010

Golden Rule, Ad Version: Speak unto others as you wo
9:10 am Jan 12th 2010

If your single most persuasive idea takes more than c
6:48 am Jan 14th 2010

Best to be relevant and interesting. But if you err, err on
7:35 am Jan 15th 2010

Fortune favors the bold over the boldfaced. Wr
9:36 am Jan 18th 2010

Money is rarely a creative's sole motivation. But don't mist
6:55 am Jan 19th 2010

r remaining 10%-bigger logos to charity in your name.

creating it.

e them speak unto you.

ntence to explain, it probably isn't single. Or persuasive.

e of interesting.

cordingly.

r being of no motivation.

If you can't say why it's wrong,
don't say that it's wrong

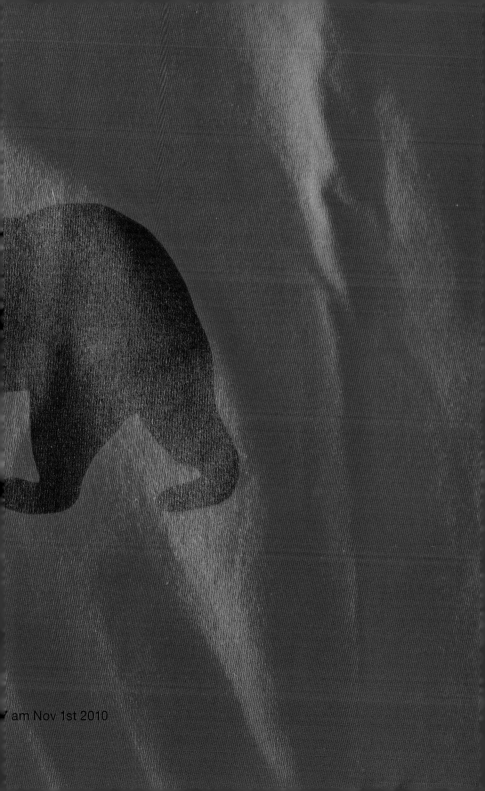

am Nov 1st 2010

A brand doesn't need a unique position in
the market as much as a unique position in
consumers' minds.
6:50 am Dec 17th 2009

The Next Big Thing is rarely discovered by
people looking for The Next Big Thing.
9:34 am Dec 18th 2009

Always assume no one wants to hear
what your ad has to say, then give them
a reason to.
7:53 am Dec 21st 2009

There's a place where copywriters never
use the phrase "there's a place." It's called
"in my presence."
7:41 am Dec 28th 2009

This copy is not...dramatic.
9:04 am Dec 29th 2009

As in life, advertising isn't about having
something worth saying, it's about having
something worth hearing.
11:42 am Jan 1st 2010

9:42 am Nov 10th 2010

A long copy ad is a great test for any writer. Lorem ipsum dolor sit amet
do eiusmod tempor incididunt ut labore et dolore magna aliqua. Ut e
exercitation ullamco laboris nisi ut aliquip ex ea commodo consequa
derit in voluptate velit esse cillum dolore eu fugiat nulla pariatur. Exce
proident, sunt in culpa qui officia deserunt mollit anim id est laborum
natus error sit voluptatem accusantium doloremque laudantium, tot
ab illo inventore veritatis et quasi architecto beatae vitae dicta sunt e
tatem quia voluptas sit aspernatur aut odit aut fugit, sed quia conse
cione voluptatem sequi nesciunt. Neque porro quisquam est, qui d
consectetur, adipisci velit, sed quia non numquam eius modi tempo
nam aliquam quaerat voluptatem. Ut enim ad minima veniam, quis
poris suscipit laboriosam, nisi ut aliquid ex ea commodi consequat
nenderit qui in ea voluptate velit esse quam nihil molestiae consequa
quo voluptas nulla pariatur? At vero eos et accusamus et iusto odio
praesentium voluptatum deleniti atque corrupti quos dolores et quas
cupiditate non provident, similique sunt in culpa qui officia deseru
dolorum fuga. Et harum quidem rerum facilis est et expedita distinct
nobis est eligendi optio cumque nihil impedit quo minus id quod ma
nis voluptas assumenda est, omnis dolor repellendus. Temporibu
debitis aut rerum necessitatibus saepe eveniet ut et voluptates rep
cusandae. Itaque earum rerum hic tenetur a sapiente delectus, ut a
alias consequatur aut perferendis doloribus asperiores repellat. Lo
retur adipisicing elit, sed do eiusmod tempor incididunt ut labore e
minim veniam, quis nostrud exercitation ullamco laboris nisi ut aliqu
aute irure dolor in reprehenderit in voluptate velit esse cillum dolore
sint occaecat cupidatat non proident, sunt in culpa qui officia dese
ut perspiciatis unde omnis iste natus error sit voluptatem accusant
rem aperiam, eaque ipsa quae ab illo inventore veritatis et quasi ar
plicabo. Nemo enim ipsam voluptatem quia voluptas sit aspernatu
quuntur magni dolores eos qui ratione voluptatem sequi nesciunt.
orem ipsum quia dolor sit amet, consectetur, adipisci velit, sed quia
ncidunt ut labore et dolore magnam aliquam quaerat voluptatem. L
crum exercitationem ullam corporis suscipit laboriosam, nisi ut aliquic
autem vel eum iure reprehenderit qui in ea voluptate velit esse quan
um qui dolorem eum fugiat quo voluptas nulla pariatur? At vero eos
simos ducimus qui blanditiis praesentium voluptatum deleniti atc
molestias excepturi sint occaecati cupiditate non provident, similiq
mollitia animi, id est laborum et dolorum fuga. Et harum quidem rer
Nam libero tempore, cum soluta nobis est eligendi optio cumque n
me placeat facere possimus, omnis voluptas assumenda est, omni
cess sint itatibus omnis est saepe evenieuio lisoseit **And an e**

sectetur adipisicing elit, sed
minim veniam, quis nostrud
aute irure dolor in reprehen
sint occaecat cupidatat non
perspiciatis unde omnis iste
n aperiam, eaque ipsa quae
o. Nemo enim ipsam volup-
ur magni dolores eos qui ra-
ipsum quia dolor sit amet,
dunt ut labore et dolore mag
m exercitatio nem ullam cor
is autem vel eum iure repre
illum qui dolorem eum fugiat
simos ducimus qui blanditiis
cias excepturi sint occae cati
itia animi, id est laborum et
libero tempore, cum soluta
laceat facere possimus, om
m quibusdam et aut officiis
dae sint et molestiae non re
en dis voluptatibus maiores
sum dolor sit amet, consec
e magna aliqua. Ut enim ad
commodo consequat. Duis
iat nulla pariatur. Excepteur
llit anim id est laborum Sed
premque laudantium, totam
o beatae vitae dicta sunt ex
it aut fugit, sed quia conse
porro quisquam est, qui do
umquam eius modi tempora
ad minima veniam, quis nos
ommodi consequatur? Quis
olestiae consequatur, vel il-
samus et iusto odio dignis-
rupti quos dolores et quas
n culpa qui officia deserunt
is est et expedita distinctio.
dit quo minus id quod max
epe llendus. Taut rerum ne-
ter one for an art director. 7:45 am Jun 30th 2010

ENDING WORL

"CHALL

OCCASIONALLY

CLIENT HE'S V

"YOUR

8:14 am Apr 9th 2010
HUNGER IS A
ENGE”
TELLING YOUR
RONG IS JUST
JOB”

Shocking is easy. Shockingly brilliant, a bit more challenging.

8:03 am Jul 23rd 2010

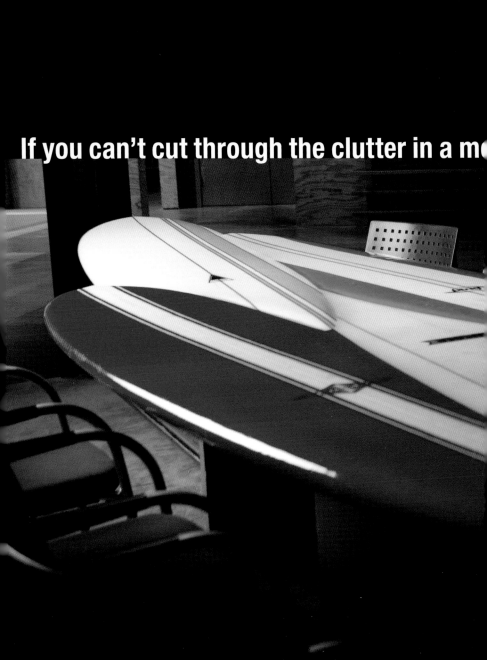

If you can't cut through the clutter in a m

ıg, how do you expect to do so in public?

When concepting, it's best to get as many people as possible into one room. And then go somewhere else.

11:06 am Nov 3rd 2009

on collaboration]

ust because all opinions are welcome doesn't
nean all opinions are valid. Now stop pouting.

No consumer woke up today thinking, "I can't wait for some proactive brand engagement."
8:22 am Sep 3rd 2010

Do not confuse purity of design with purity of message. One can make some remarkably stupid ideas look breathtaking.
8:34 am Sep 7th 2010

The way to a brand's heart is through your gut.
8:00 am Sep 8th 2010

Never say something is "this and that" if "that" is the same as "this." Got that?
8:22 am Sep 9th 2010

Standing over the art director's shoulder and sighing at her font choice does not qualify as "managing the process."
8:01 am Sep 15th 2010

Many folks who seem bent on "managing the process" have little idea what the process actually is.
8:16 am Sep 17th 2010

If your work doesn't reflect your strategy and insights, you should probably stop touting your strategic insightfulness.
8:26 am Sep 20th 2010

If you insist on spending millions of dollars to go unnoticed, buy a stealth fighter, not an ad campaign.
8:23 am Sep 21st 2010

Unless your targets are 18th century French dandies, save flowery language for open mic poetry night.
8:26 am Sep 23rd 2010

Big ideas are often only deemed such after the fact.
The fact being that they were actually produced.
8:11 am Sep 24th 2010

Keep it moving, folks – it's a status meeting, not a
stasis meeting.
8:48 am Sep 27th 2010

If it doesn't work as a pencil sketch, tarting it up with
fancy production values won't save it.
8:33 am Sep 28th 2010

Aiming straight down the middle often results in home runs.
For the competition.
8:24 am Sep 29th 2010

A fun phrase to start a status meeting: Just because you
caved to pacify the client, doesn't mean I'll cave to pacify you.
8:18 am Sep 30th 2010

Dear Jr. AE, I see your desire to sound smart defeated your
desire to be understood. Sadly, we all lost. Love, LCB
8:13 am Oct 1st 2010

It is possible to be too direct, too transparent and too simple.
Few people want to marry a blunt, loquacious hillbilly.
9:05 am Oct 4th 2010

You don't have to know a brand inside-out to turn its fortunes
right-side up. You just have to know its customers.
8:21 am Oct 6th 2010

GOOD CLIENTS
PAY
THE

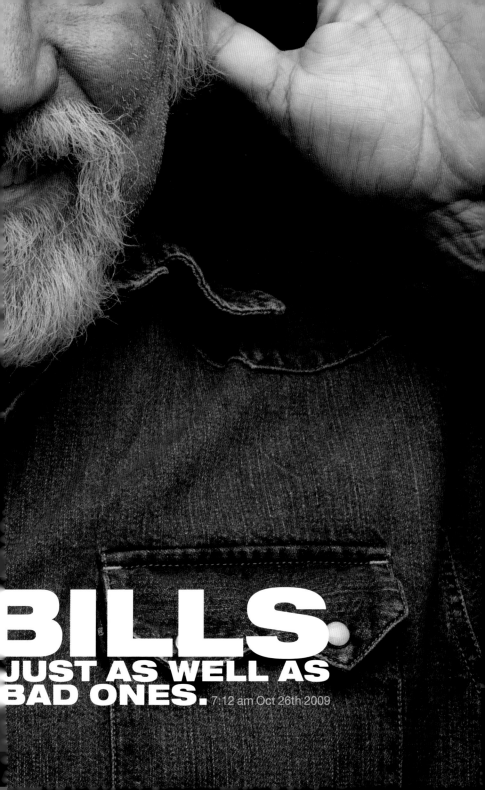

BILLS.
JUST AS WELL AS
BAD ONES. 7:12 am Oct 26th 2009

BRANDS MOVE FORWARD WHEN BRA

WHAT IS AND STARTS INSPIRING

2010 "I LIKE THE WAY YOU THINK" I

WAY YOUR WORK MAKES ME THINK

2010 INSPIRATION IS RANDOM. CRE

22ND 2010 NEVER USE TWO ADJE

AM DEC 27TH 2010 SIMPLICITY W

A QUICKER PATH TO BOREDOM. 9

OF "WE JUST HAVE TO DO SOMET

DOES NOTHING. WELL, AT LEAST NO

EVERY PROJECT IS NOT AN OPPO

PROJECT CAN BE A CHANCE TO H

2010 THE ONLY THING DUMBING

WAS ATTRACTING MORE DUMB PE

NEVER NEED PERMISSION TO BE

DEAREST MANAGEMENT, IF AN

AHEAD AND ACTUALLY CELEBRATE I

ADVERTISING STOPS REINFORCING

AT COULD BE. 8:15 AM DEC 20TH

GREAT COMPLIMENT. "I LIKE THE

GREATER STILL. 8:32 AM DEC 21ST

VITY, PREMEDITATED. 7:57 AM DEC

VES WHERE NONE WILL DO. 8:45

OUT ELEGANCE MERELY CREATES

O AM DEC 28TH 2010 A STRATEGY

G" OFTEN RESULTS IN WORK THAT

ING GOOD. 11:22 PM DEC 29TH 2010

UNITY FOR GREATNESS, BUT ANY

E YOUR CRAFT. 9:06 AM DEC 30TH

N AN IDEA EVER ACCOMPLISHED

E. 8:36 AM DEC 31ST 2010 YOU

RESTING. 8:22 AM JAN 3RD 2011

A IS WORTH CELEBRATING, GO

OVE, LCB 8:58 PM JAN 13TH 2011

7:46 am Aug 6th 2010

Successful collaboration does not require a single committee.

8:15 am Dec 17th 201

People should be able to spot your work because it's consistently great. Not consistently the same.

AWARD SHOW JUDGING IS OFTEN RANDOM AND CAPRICIOU
JUST LIKE REAL CONSUMER BEHAVIOR. 7:50 AM FEB 24TH 20
IT IS MORE IMPORTANT TO HAVE LIKABLE CREATIVE THA
LIKABLE CREATIVES. 8:11 AM MAR 3RD 2010 TIGHTWADS RARE
INSPIRE ANYTHING BUT RESENTMENT. 7:30 AM MAR 4TH 20
ONE SHOULD ALWAYS BE SENSITIVE TO A CLIENT'S NEEDS AI
PREFERENCES WHEN EXPLAINING WHY THEY DON'T MATTER
CONSUMERS. 7:49 AM MAR 5TH 2010 DON'T EXPECT PEOPLE
THINK ABOVE THEIR PAY GRADE IF YOU PAY THEM BELOW
7:17 AM MAR 9TH 2010 DO NOT MISTAKE CONVICTION F(
STUBBORNNESS. OR, JUST AS IMPORTANTLY, THE INVERS
7:23 AM MAR 10TH 2010 CONSENSUS PUTS THE "C" IN "CYA." A
NOT IN A GOOD WAY. 7:52 AM MAR 11TH 2010 NEVER PUT C
UNTIL TOMORROW WHAT YOU CAN KILL TODAY. 7:46 AM M
12TH 2010 DURABLE MEDICAL GOODS EXCEPTED, NO ONE NEE
YOUR BRAND AS MUCH AS YOU NEED THEM TO NEED YO
BRAND. TRY NOT TO ACT DESPERATE. 7:47 AM MAR 15TH 20
IF YOUR MAIN CLIENT CONTACT CAN'T MAKE DECISION
HE OR SHE SHOULDN'T BE YOUR MAIN CLIENT CONTA
8:15 AM MAR 16TH 2010 DEAREST CLIENT, WE'LL START BUYI
MOST OF YOUR PRODUCT. LOVE LCB 7:22 AM MAR 18TH 2

No one remembers boring ads.

But they never forget how boring your brand is. 8:15 am Oct 25th 2010

People want it faster, better, in a different color and f
I now declare all focus groups moot. 6:48 am Feb 1st 2010

ee (with free shipping).

8:00 am Oct 29th 2010

CRITICIZING
EVERYTHING
THAT CROSSES
YOUR DESK
DOES NOT
QUALIFY YOU
AS A CRITICAL
THINKER.

I prefer psychographics to demographics.
Partly because they're more useful.
Partly because they sound dangerous.

7:58 am Apr 21st 2010

LIKE THE WORLD IN GENERAL, ADVERTISING NEEDS FEWER GURUS AND MORE VISIONARIES. 7:54 am Oct 8th 2010

WHILE ANYONE CAN BE CREATIVE, REAL CREATIVES CAN BE NOTHING BUT. LUCKY US. 8:08 am Oct 13th 2010

THE DUMBEST CONSUMER CAN EASILY OUTWIT THE SMARTEST BRAND MANAGER. OR CREATIVE DIRECTOR. SIGH. 8:13 am Oct 18th 2010

DEAREST CLIENT, IN THE END, CHEAP WORK COSTS YOU PLENTY. LOVE, LCB 8:45 am Nov 18th 2010

IF MEETINGS SOLVED PROBLEMS, THE WORLD WOULD'VE ACHIEVED UTOPIA ON AUGUST 14, 1973. 7:57 am Nov 26th 2010

STOP PUTTING THE WORK NUMBER ONE AND YOU'LL SOON BE DEEP IN NUMBER TWO. 7:57 am Dec 3rd 2010

NEVER TRUST AN AGENCY THAT CAN'T FIGURE OUT ITS OWN BRAND. 8:20 am Dec 6th 2010

NEVER START A CONVERSATION WITH A YAWN. 8:12 am Jan 5th 2011

SIMPLICITY IS USUALLY THE RESULT OF MUCH COMPLEX THINKING. 8:06 am Jan 7th 2011

IT'S NOT CAUTION WE'RE THROWING TO THE WIND, IT'S FEAR. 8:15 am Mar 30th 2011

WIDE-RANGING APPEAL OFTEN COMES FROM A NARROWLY FOCUSED MESSAGE. 9:18 am Jan 19th 2011

A WRITER WHO THINKS VISUALLY IS GREAT. A WRITER WHOSE WORDS MAKE OTHERS THINK VISUALLY, EVEN BETTER. 8:28 am Jan 25th 2011

KEEP IT SIMPLE, STRATEGIST. 8:03 am Jan 27th 2011

PLAY IT SMART AND THE CLIENT WON'T WORRY ABOUT PLAYING IT SAFE. 8:54 am Feb 3rd 2011

SOMETIMES THE BEST WAY TO COLLABORATE IS TO SIMPLY GET OUT OF THE WAY. 8:20 am Feb 8th 2011

WHAT AN AD DOES IS MORE IMPORTANT THAN WHAT IT SAYS. 8:10 am Feb 11th 2011

IMAGINE WHAT COULD BE, DISCERN WHAT SHOULD BE, THEN HELP MAKE IT BE. 8:26 am Feb 15th 2011

REAL THOUGHT LEADERS LEAD BY DOING. 8:21 am Feb 22nd 2011

NO CONSUMER WILL EVER JUDGE AN AD ON HOW WELL IT BUILT INTERNAL CONSENSUS. 8:05 am Feb 24th 2011

JUST BECAUSE IT'S MEASURABLE DOESN'T MEAN IT MATTERS. 8:10 am Mar 8th 2011

SOMETIMES THE BEST VISUAL SOLUTION IS A WELL-WRITTEN LINE.

6:42 am Aug 25th 2009

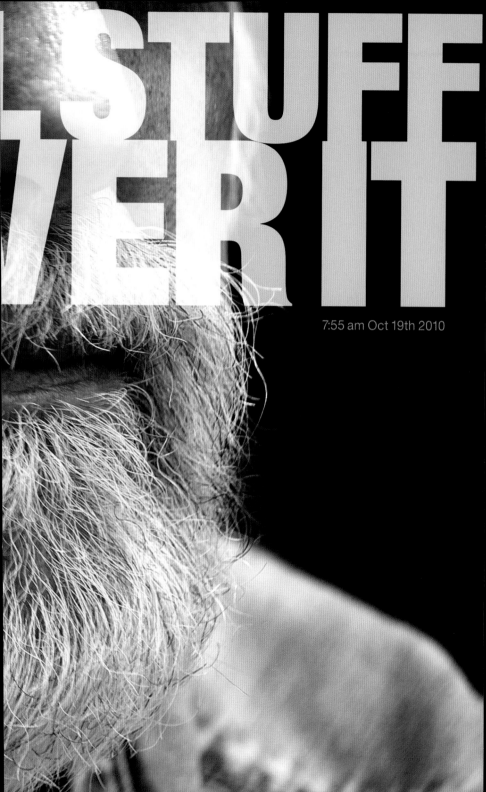

STUFF
VERIT

7:55 am Oct 19th 2010

History rarely remembers a critic.

6:19 am May 25th 2009

Consumers want relevant communication.
They don't care if it's the Next Big Media Thing or
a re-aired Shake 'n Bake spot.
7:16 am Jun 1st 2009

Dearest Wonk, your use of jargon betrays your
lack of insight.
6:26 am Jun 2nd 2009

Few things are more embarrassing than letting an
ad out in public with its strategy showing.
8:12 am Jun 3rd 2009

Body copy gets read when headlines do their job.
6:12 am Jun 4th 2009

Everyone really is a copywriter, art director, etc.
So go on. Be better than everyone.
10:05 am Jun 5th 2009

Most products don't actually have a USP.
That's why *we* exist.
9:22 am Jun 8th 2009

New does not necessarily equal good. Old does not
necessarily equal bad. Exercise wisdom accordingly.
9:28 am Jun 9th 2009

Try being inspired by the world around you. Better to
rip off God than CA.
7:22 am Jun 12th 2009

Hey, remember that really boring ad

moved a ton of product? Neither do I.

8:38 am Jul 6th 2010

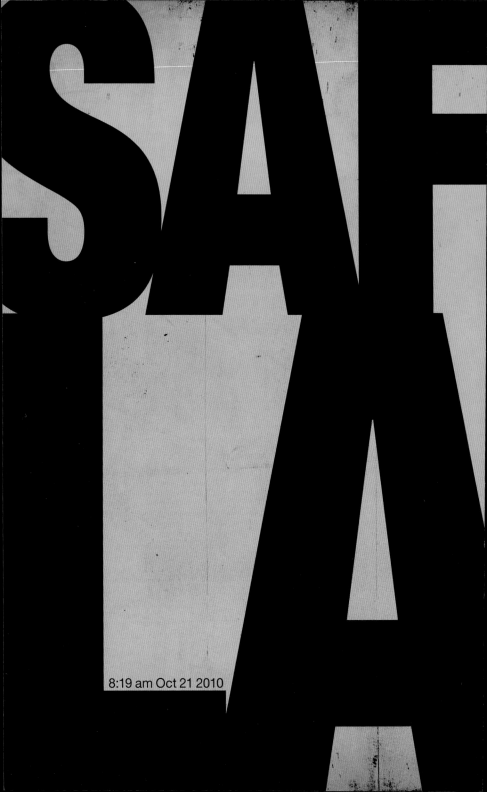

8:19 am Oct 21 2010

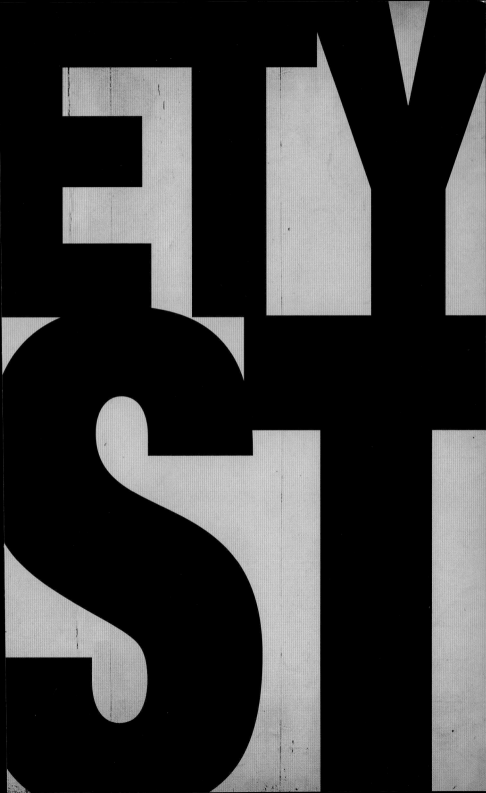

Make it smart.
Make it beautiful.
Have fun.

Lee

One day I was in the office and someone said to me, "Hey Lee, I loved your tweet this morning on Lee Clow's Beard."

That was weird.

Because I don't tweet. And what does my beard have to do with it?

Months went by. And within those months I'd often hear, "Hey Lee, that tweet you said today was so true."

Again, it wasn't me. I don't tweet. I say smart stuff now and again. But I'm not sitting around trying to figure out how to make my words fit into 140 characters.

It became somewhat of a mystery. We were all trying to figure who it was. Was it one of my old partners? Or someone who worked at the agency? I mostly liked the thoughts in the tweets, I just didn't tweet them.

Then one day Rob discovered the truth.

It turns out that there was a kid in Texas. He had his own smart stuff to say about ads, clients, what pisses us off and makes us happy. And it was stuff that I would have said. It's stuff that I've heard passionate ad guys say all the time.

That kid is named Jason Fox. We flew him out to LA. I wanted to meet him. We had lunch. And well, one thing led to another and we decided to put this book together.

So, while I may not have technically tweeted these tweets, I certainly believe they are truisms. In fact, I've approved them coming from my beard. Jason told me at lunch that he had to make a choice when he started his daily observations. You could have been reading this advertising wisdom from "Jeff Goodby's Ponytail."

Love,

When I first logged on to Twitter in April 2009 with the purpose of satirizing the ad industry and deflating the guru-centric world of social media, my intended nom de tweet was not @leeclowsbeard. However, circumstances and squatters' rights soon shifted my attention to Lee—a man I had, like many in our industry, long admired, never met and knew little about. As a lack of knowledge had yet to hinder any ad man, I forged on.

After a few tentative, mostly hobo-related jokes about being an anthropomorphized beard, I realized any hopes for longevity—and followers—demanded a new tack. Zagging from the snark oozing through 99.99% of the Internet, I decided to be as wise as my user name implied. Or at least fake it as well as I could. And so began the tweet-a-day offering of advertising-related crumbs I had theoretically accumulated through the years while keeping Lee's chin warm and his soup on instant replay.

Slowly the followers came, including Rob Schwartz, Chiat's L.A.-based Chief Creative Officer. Not wanting to open a can of cease-and-desist orders, I refrained from harassment for almost a year. When I finally inquired as to Lee's knowledge of LCB, Rob confirmed that he was aware of my existence, and that he approved of my hijinks. Huzzah.

A couple of months later, Rob and Lee flew me out for a lunch that was, from my perspective, a very "one of these things is not like the other" moment. But both men were exceedingly gracious and moderately impressed with my growing legion of Beardists, which had cracked the 10,000 mark the day prior. Somewhere between the soup and the sushi, the idea for this book was born.

I hope as few people as possible are disappointed to discover that some unknown Midwesterner is really the chin behind the whiskers. But in a way, that (unintended) deception is the point—to prove that smart people inhabit every corner of the advertising world. After all, not everyone gets a shot working at well-known shops for deep-pocketed clients. Some of us have to convince elderly folks to prearrange services at discount funeral homes, as I did at my first job.

I realize LCB is akin to preaching to the choir. And that's okay. Because while the choir may already agree with what the pastor is preaching, they need some inspiration for the daily grind, too. I hope to have provided that in some small way. At least enough to get folks through the next status meeting or conference call.

As with any worthwhile endeavor, thanks are in order. To God for, among other more significant things, giving me this talent as recompense for my pasty afro. To my wife, Megan, for putting up with a melancholy writer-type. To my kids, Gideon, Charlotte and Simon, who give daddy a reason to face the daily slog. To my parents for never asking why they spent so much money on a business degree when a nice pen and pencil set would have sufficed. To my art director partners through the years — collaborators and co-conspirators all. To the colleagues who taught me what advertising should and should not be. To Rob Schwartz for spearheading this effort when he had 3,956 more important projects to oversee. To Bill Hornstein for his outstanding book design. To, of course, Lee Clow for loaning out his beardiness and inspiring us all in an industry where inspiration is often spoken of but rarely delivered. And finally, to every person who clicked that "follow" button and made this book possible.

May you all grow long and prosper.

Jason Fox
Dallas, Texas
March 2011

THX.

Emmanuel André, Carisa Bianchi, Jigisha Bouverat, Laurel Burden, Senna Chen, Lee Clow, Craig Cohen, Linda Daubson, Wes Del Val, Nick Drake, Laurie Fisher, Jason Fox, Stan Frgacic, Jennifer Golub, Neal Grossman, Bob Hezlep, Paul Hiroto, Bill Hornstein, Katherine Howells, Rick Legoretta, Will Luckman, Kristen McCoy, Jeremy Miller, Casey Mooney, Hugo Muñoz, Darren Murray, Barbara Overlie, Michele Pappas, Kat Pingol, Krzysztof Poluwicz, Daniel Power, Scott Roberts, Juan Salazar, Rob Schwartz, Jimmy Smith, Kerri Sparkman, Marianne Stefanowicz, Elaine Stein, Yin Ulmen, Nina Ventura, Josh Withers.

Photographers: Emmanuel André, Lee Clow, Richard Corman, Laura Crosta, Stephanie Diani, Bill Hornstein, Tammy Kennedy, Ron Krisel.

Illustrator: Hank Hinton

Text © 2012 @leeclowsbeard

Page 3, 16, 59, 68, 73, 89, 100, 126-127, 166, photograph source unknown
Page 6-7, photograph by Bill Hornstein of illustration © Hank Hinton
Page 9, 12-13, 26, 34-35, 38-39, 42-43, 64-65, 98-99, 106-107, 118-119, 120-121, 128-129, 130-131,
132-133, 135, 136-137, 138-139, 144-145, 150-151, 152, 158-159, 164-165, 172-173, 176-177, 190-191,
196-197, 200-201, 206-207, 210-211, 216, photographs © Bill Hornstein
Page 20-21, 115, 124-125, Lee Clow's personal photographs
Page 24-25, photograph © Laura Crosta
Page 30-31, 184-185, photographs © Emmanuel André
Page 46, 52-53, 60-61, 77, 87, 108-109, 140, 156-157, 178-179, photographs © Ron Krisel
Page 80-81, 92-93, 214, photographs © Stephanie Diani
Page 82-83, photograph of illustration by Lee Clow © Bill Hornstein
Page 108-109, photograph © Bill Hornstein of photograph by Ron Krisel
Page 146-147, photograph © TBWA\Chiat\Day

Published in the United States by powerHouse Books,
a division of powerHouse Cultural Entertainment, Inc.
37 Main Street, Brooklyn, NY 11201-1021
telephone 212.604.9074, fax 212.366.5247
e-mail: leeclowsbeard@powerhousebooks.com
website: www.powerhousebooks.com

First edition, 2012

Library of Congress Control Number: 2011936827

Hardcover ISBN 978-1-57687-605-3

Printing and binding by RR Donnelley
Book design by Bill Hornstein

A complete catalog of powerHouse Books and Limited Editions is available upon request;
please call, write, or visit our website.

10 9 8 7 6 5 4 3 2 1

Printed and bound in China

FSC
www.fsc.org
MIX
Paper from
responsible sources
FSC® C101537